How to
Be a Diva

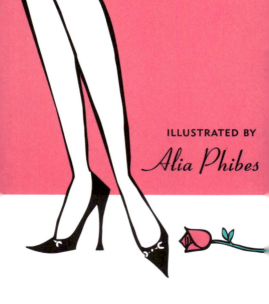

ILLUSTRATED BY

Alia Phibes

How to Be a Diva

MARY CARNAHAN

ARIEL BOOKS

Andrews McMeel Publishing

Kansas City

ISBN: 0-7407-4211-6
Library of Congress Catalog Card Number: 2003111539

How to
Be a Diva

ASK YOURSELF THIS QUESTION:

Do you secretly
suspect that

the world revolves around

you?

HAVE LESSER MORTALS ACCUSED YOU

OF **"RUNNING ROUGHSHOD"** OVER THEM

(as if you would

wear anything but

the most trendy, exquisite,

designer footwear!)?

Well,
brace yourself.

YOU MAY BE A

Diva.

JACK UP

YOUR

THRONE,

WOMAN.

You

ARE A

goddess.

LESSER MORTALS
may occasionally refer to you as

"Bitch,"

but you can't expect them

to see things from

your perspective.

The

Diva life

is a

good one,

BUT DEMANDING.

So many shoes,

so many hairstyles,

so little time.

BUT YOU ARE UP TO IT.

You are a

take-charge kinda girl,

a Fashion-Mag Do

in the flesh.

any dictionary

will tell you, comes

from

divine.

DIVAHOOD ✓

IS NOT SO MUCH A STYLE AS AN

INALIENABLE RIGHT.

However, the basics of
Divahood are as follows:

attitude,

attitude,

attitude.

AND

I DO MEAN

ATTITUDE

WITH A

CAPITAL

Go stand in front of the mirror,

preferably on a

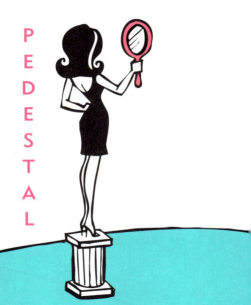

PEDESTAL

Affect a confident,

almost insolent stance.

Stand up straight,
for God's sake,

take a breath,

and then relax

ever so slightly into an

attitude of bored,

seen-it-all readiness.

Your look of Utter Conviction
is your best tool.

Lower your eyelids,

gaze at mirror-girl,

and say, as if you have

Better Things to Do, "What–?"

"No, I was here first,"

"And your point is–?"

and, more important,

"PUT THAT ON MY ACCOUNT."

You know, in your bones,

that you are

IT

—THE BOMB,

THE ONE,

THE CEO OF

ALL YOU SURVEY.

You are so worthy.

The difference between being a Diva and merely being vain is that

You're a Diva if, just walking down the street, you are flanked by followers attracted like human metal filings to your

intense magnetic charm.

You are surrounded by your retinue.

Worshiped,
adored,
cherished

by the crowd. . . .

No, not just any crowd.

The crowd

that spends money.

The crowd that lunches.

But is it

THE CHANEL SUIT,

THE DIAMONDS,

THE ROLEX,

THE BEEMER?

That definable something? NO.

It's not the number of shoes,
or the many outfits specially made
just for you at House of Ostentation.

Awaken and arise,
secure in the knowledge that
**no one in the land is
more fascinating than**

It's not
the accessories.
It's the fact
that you were ·············

you.

Bathe in
something fitting,

such as

champagne.

Anoint yourself

with fine jewels,

·····➤ *Born to*

Wear

Them.

Hey. It's your birthright.

You are a high maintenance,

bona fide bombshell.

clothing, and scent.

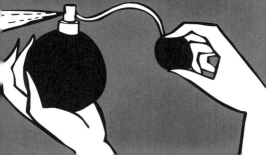

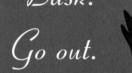

Bask.

Go out.

RULE.

Art direction & design
by **BTDnyc**

This book
was set in Geometric
and Coronet.

You are the

Alpha Babe.

Your Past Life
résumé would read
something like this:

Eve,

Delilah,

Cleopatra,

Mona Lisa,

YOU HAVE EARNED
THE RIGHT TO BE

this

wonderful

You,

and you may
as well enjoy it,
unflinchingly.

*To begin with, every day is a day
to do Something Extra Nice for you.
After all, your patron saint is*

**OUR LADY OF
HIGH MAINTENANCE.**